PIANO ACCOMPANIMENT

FOR CHURCH

AMY ADAM
MIKE HANNICKEL

CURNOW® MUSIC

EXCLUSIVELY DISTRIBUTED BY
HAL•LEONARD® CORPORATION
7777 W. BLUEMOUND RD. P.O. BOX 13819 MILWAUKEE, WI 53213

Edition Number: CMP 0869-03-401

Amy Adam, Mike Hannickel
TONS OF TUNES for Church
Piano Accompaniment

ISBN 978-90-431-1981-8

ARRANGERS

MIKE HANNICKEL grew up in the Sacramento, California area and attended California State University, Sacramento and the University of Southern California. He has been a music teacher in Rocklin, California since 1973. He also composes and publishes exclusively with Curnow Music Press, with whom he has dozens of pieces of music in print.

AMY ADAM was raised in Grand Rapids, Minnesota and attended the University of Minnesota, Duluth graduating with a BM in band education and Flute performance. She has been a music teacher in California since 1992 and currently teaches in Rocklin, California.

TONS OF TUNES

TONS OF TUNES FOR CHURCH is filled with fun and familiar pieces that musicians love to play. All the songs have been arranged in easy keys for wind instruments. The **professional quality accompaniment CD** can be used for practice and performance.

TO THE MUSIC TEACHER OR CHURCH MUSIC DIRECTOR:
TONS OF TUNES for CHURCH is a great way to help get young musicians actively involved in your church music program. Every tune in the book can be performed with the CD accompaniment or with the Piano/Organ book. All **TONS OF TUNES for CHURCH** books can be used alone or together so a variety of small ensembles can be created. Whether for prelude, offertory, church social, talent show or any other gathering, **TONS OF TUNES for CHURCH** is just what you need. Chord symbols are provided in the Piano accompaniment book for Keyboard, Guitar and combo use.

TO THE MUSICIAN:
Have **FUN** playing these songs alone or with your family and friends! Even if you have different instruments, you can still play together. Each person needs to get the **TONS OF TUNES FOR CHURCH** book for their instrument.

FOR CHURCH
CONTENTS

TONS OF TUNES FOR CHURCH
1. ABIDE WITH ME

Amy Adam (ASCAP) and
Mike Hannickel (ASCAP)

2. NOW THANK WE ALL OUR GOD

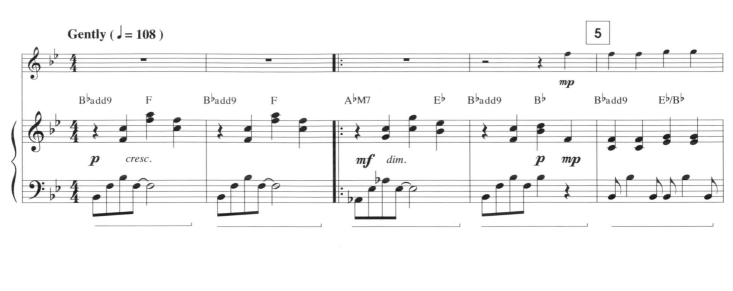

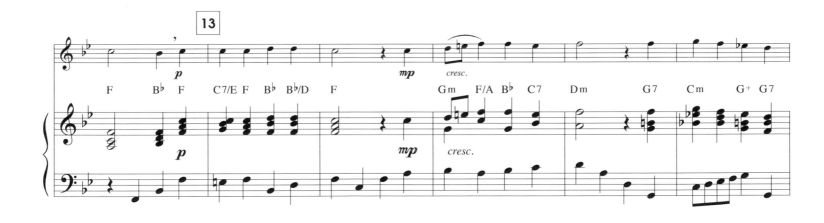

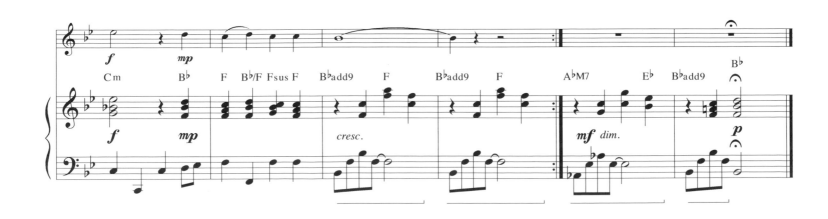

0869.03 CMP • *Piano Accompaniment*

3. DO, LORD

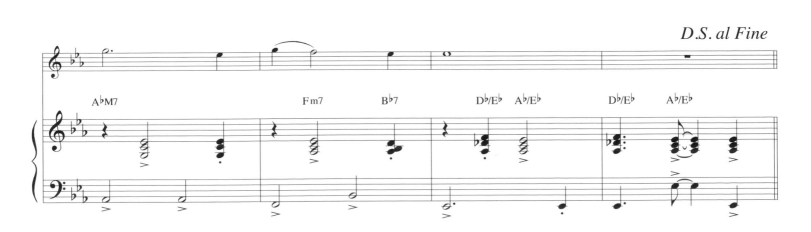

4. BEAUTIFUL SAVIOR

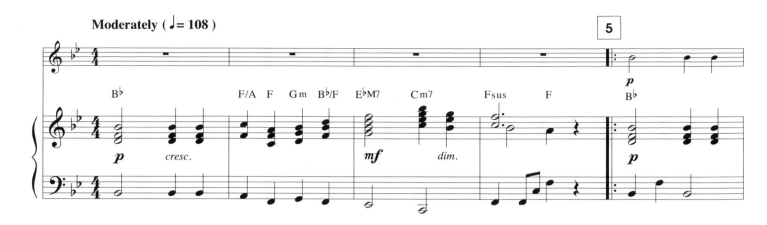

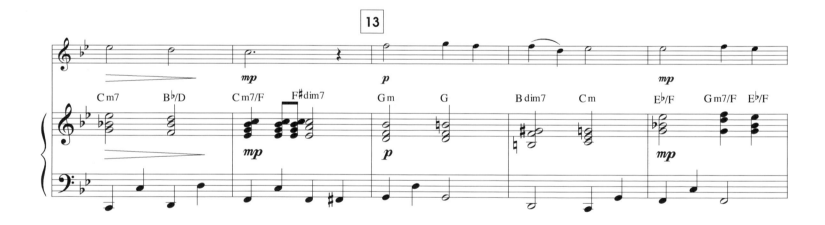

5. FOR THE BEAUTY OF THE EARTH

0869.03 CMP • Piano Accompaniment

6. HOLY, HOLY, HOLY

7. JESUS LOVES ME

0869.03 CMP • Piano Accompaniment

8. MY FAITH LOOKS UP TO THEE

13

9. JUST AS I AM

Tenderly (♩ = 102)

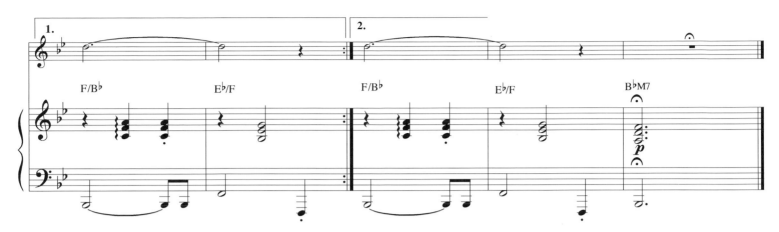

10. CROWN HIM WITH MANY CROWNS

Majestically (♩ = 102)

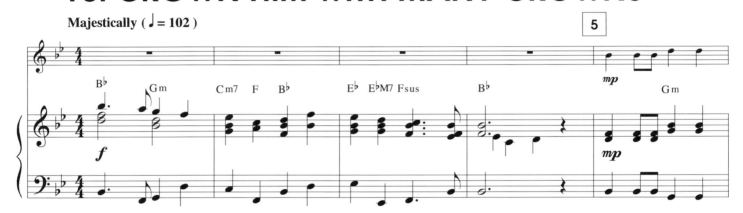

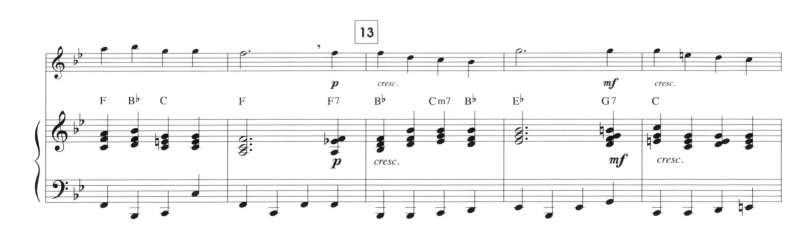

11. COME, THOU ALMIGHTY KING

Moderately (♩ = 112)

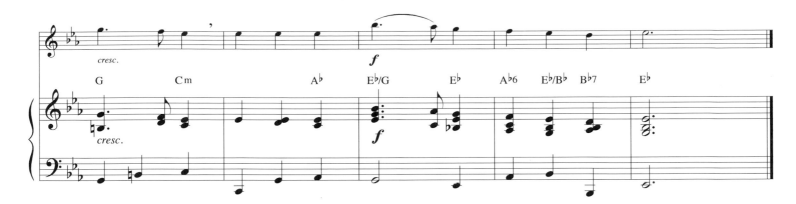

12. OH, WON'T YOU SIT DOWN?

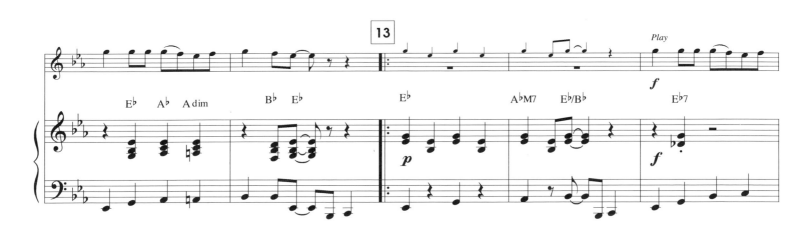

13. O FOR A THOUSAND TONGUES

Moderately (♩ = 108)

　　　　　　　　　　　　　　　　　　　　　　　　　　　　　0869.03 CMP • Piano Accompaniment

19

14. CHILDREN OF THE HEAVENLY FATHER

Lightly (♩ = 102)

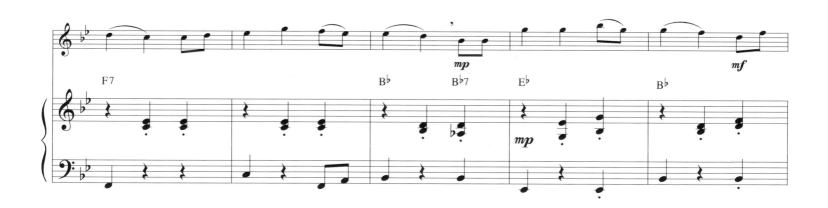

15. THE CHURCH'S ONE FOUNDATION

16. NEARER MY GOD TO THEE

Gently, with emotion (♩ = 96)

17. PRAISE TO THE LORD, THE ALMIGHTY

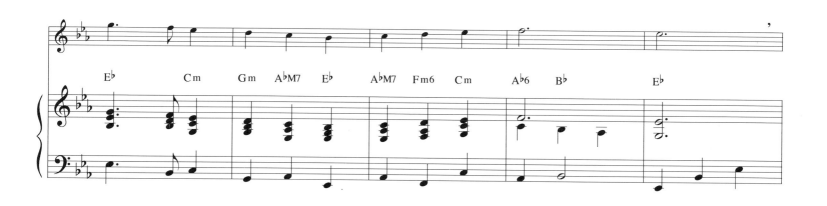

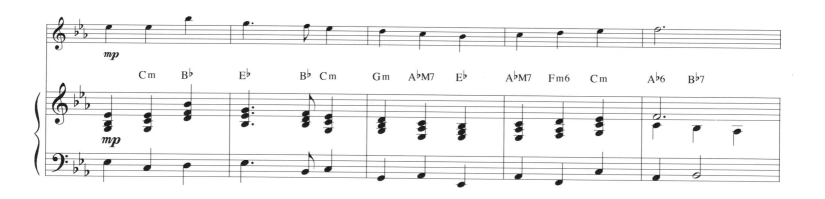

18. ALL GLORY, LAUD AND HONOR

Moderately (♩ = 102)

19. ALL HAIL THE POWER

With energy (♩ = 132)

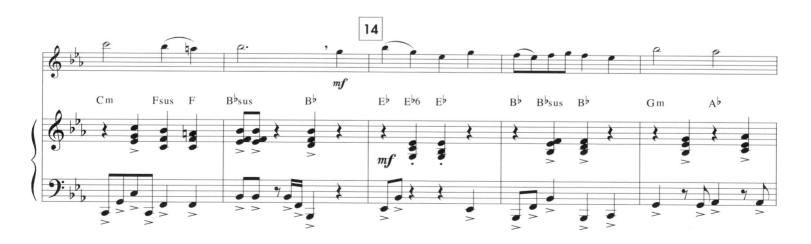

20. GOD OF GRACE AND GOD OF GLORY

Moderately (♩ = 108)

21. SWING LOW, SWEET CHARIOT

Moderately (♩=108)

27

22. HE'S GOT THE WHOLE WORLD IN HIS HANDS

23. GO TELL IT ON THE MOUNTAIN

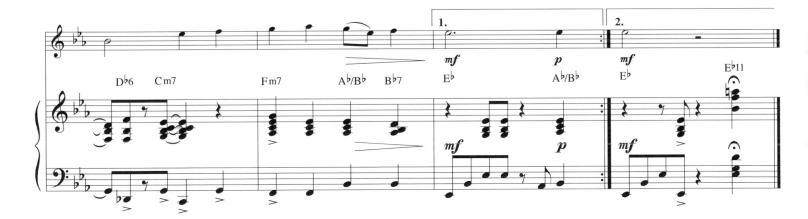

24. THIS TRAIN

25. WHAT A FRIEND WE HAVE IN JESUS

Swing (♩ = 72)

26. ONWARD CHRISTIAN SOLDIERS

0869.03 CMP • Piano Accompaniment

27. IN THE SWEET BY AND BY

       0869.03 CMP • Piano Accompaniment

28. LET US BREAK BREAD TOGETHER

With spirit (♩ = 132)

29. CHRIST THE LORD IS RISEN TODAY

Majestically (♩ = 116)

37

30. WERE YOU THERE?

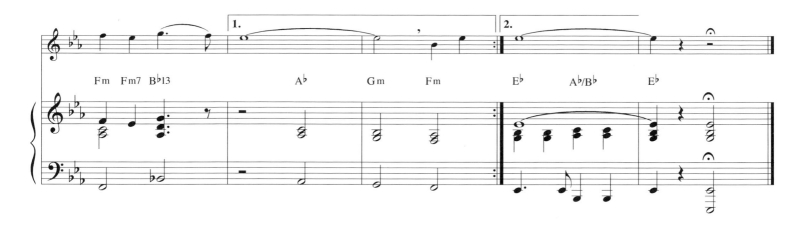

31. THIS IS MY FATHER'S WORLD

Smoothly (♩ = 96)

32. SOFTLY AND TENDERLY JESUS IS CALLING

Tenderly (♩ = 70)

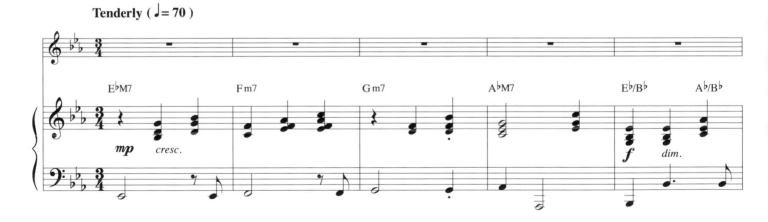

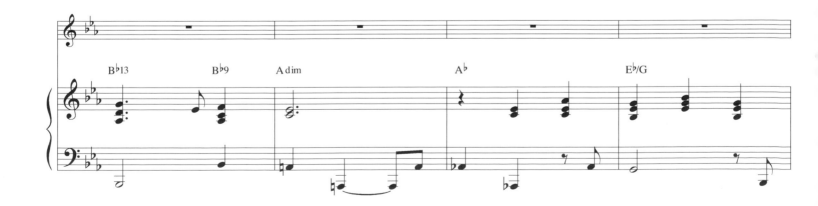